Coupon book
FOR DAD

80 GIFT COUPONS

THANK YOU
for your purchase!

We hope dad will enjoy these coupons together with you and the rest of the family.

Without your voice we cannot improve this booklet. Please support us and write us a review on Amazon or at:
lilelu.books@gmail.com

ACTIVITY COUPON

WATCH A SPORT EVENT
WITH DAD

You have to watch a sporting event with dad on TV or go together at a live event.

The coupon holder provides free popcorn and drinks.

ACTIVITY COUPON

FINISHING A PROJECT

You have to help dad finish this project.

ACTIVITY COUPON

ONE LAWN MOWING

Prepare to mow the lawn today.

FAMILY COUPON

GAME NIGHT WITH
THE ENTIRE FAMILY

Everyone should stay in and play games.

The coupon holder is responsible for organizing everything.

FAMILY COUPON

MOVIE NIGHT

Dad gets to decide what movie should the entire family watch tonight.

ACTIVITY COUPON

SPECIAL DINNER

You have to cook dad a dinner of
his choice.

Coupon holder must prepare the dish that dad wishes.

ACTIVITY COUPON

OLD FRIENDS GATHERING

Dad will spend an evening with
his buddies, at home or out.

The coupon holder must help with preparation if the
gathering happens at home.

ACTIVITY COUPON

FREE CAR WASH

Dad needs his car clean and shiny.

The coupon holder must clean dad's car.

QUIET COUPON

AN UNDISTURBED NAP

No one disturbs dad for the next
couple of hours, please!

The coupon holder takes care that no one disturbs dad.

QUIET COUPON

THREE HOURS OF

QUIETNESS

The next three hours dad needs
you to be quiet.

Must be redeemed for three hours consecutively.

QUIET COUPON

A MORNING TO SLEEP IN

This coupon must be redeemed the previous night.

The coupon holder must be sure that no one disturbs dad.

LOVE COUPON

ONE BIG HUG

Dad needs a big warm hug.

The coupon holder must give dad a warm hug.

ACTIVITY COUPON

BREAKFAST IN BED

This coupon must be redeemed the previous night.

The coupon holder must prepare dad's breakfast.

ACTIVITY COUPON

TAKING OUT THE TRASH

Dad needs you to take the trash out.

ACTIVITY COUPON

ONE HOUR OF HELP

Dad needs help with a chore of
his choice.

ACTIVITY COUPON

KEEP COMPANY
WHILE RUN ERRANDS

Dad needs your company while
driving and running errands
today.

QUIET COUPON

ONE HOUR OF UNINTERRUPTED READING TIME

Dad needs one hour to read his newspaper without being disturbed.

ACTIVITY COUPON

TWO COLD DRINKS ON A HOT DAY

Dad needs you to bring him two cold drinks regardless of what you do.

ACTIVITY COUPON

A 10-MINUTE MASSAGE

Dad needs a massage of his
choice: back, neck, feet.

FAMILY COUPON

FAMILY BONDING

Dad proposes a family activity of
his choice and everyone will
participate without complaints.

ACTIVITY COUPON

NO CHORE DAY

You have to do all dad's chores
for the day.

LOVE COUPON

A BIG KISS ON THE CHEEK

You have to give your dad a big
kiss at his wish.

ACTIVITY COUPON

TRASH WEEK

You have to take the trash out
for the entire week.

ACTIVITY COUPON

IRON THE SHIRT

You have to iron your dad's shirt.

ACTIVITY COUPON

CLEAN YOUR ROOM

You have to clean your room when your dad says so without whining.

EVERYTHING THAT HAPPENED AT SCHOOL

You have to tell your dad everything that happened at school today, without lying.

FIVE HONEST ANSWERS

You have to sincerely answer five
questions your dad asks you.

ACTIVITY COUPON

YES WEEKEND

You have to say yes to anything your dad asks you to do for an entire weekend.

ACTIVITY COUPON

ONE WEEK NO FIGHTING

You have to avoid fighting with
your siblings or your parents for
one entire week.

ACTIVITY COUPON

CLEAN THE GARAGE

Dad needs you to help him clean the garage, deposit or storage room.

FEED THE PETS FOR ONE WEEK

Dad needs you to feed any pets you have for the whole week without being reminded to do so.

ACTIVITY COUPON

NO WHINING DAYS

You have to comply and not whine
for the next three days no matter
what happens.

FAMILY COUPON

STORYTIME EVENING

Dad wants to hear at least two
stories that you never told him
about you.

ACTIVITY COUPON

CLEAN THE DISHES

You must clean the dishes the whole day after breakfast, lunch and dinner.

LOVE COUPON

ONE BIG HUG

Dad needs a big warm hug.

ACTIVITY COUPON

REMOTE CONTROL
MASTER

Dad is the remote control master
for the evening.

LOVE COUPON

A BIG KISS ON THE CHEEK

You have to give your dad a big
kiss at his wish.

ACTIVITY COUPON

A 10-MINUTE MASSAGE

Dad needs a massage of his
choice: back, neck, feet.

ACTIVITY COUPON

FREE CAR WASH

Dad needs his car squeaky clean.

The coupon holder must clean dad's car.

ACTIVITY COUPON

AN UNDISTURBED NAP

No one disturbs dad for the next
couple of hours, please!
eaky clean.

The coupon holder takes care that no one disturbs dad.

SURPRISE COUPON

_____

Dad can write anything he wants.

SURPRISE COUPON

_____

_____

_____

Dad can write anything he wants.

SURPRISE COUPON

_____

Dad can write anything he wants.

SURPRISE COUPON

_____

Dad can write anything he wants.

SURPRISE COUPON

_____

_____

_____

Dad can write anything he wants.

SURPRISE COUPON

_____

_____

_____

Dad can write anything he wants.

SURPRISE COUPON

_____

_____

_____

Dad can write anything he wants.

SURPRISE COUPON

_____

_____

_____

Dad can write anything he wants.

SURPRISE COUPON

_____

_____

_____

Dad can write anything he wants.

SURPRISE COUPON

_____

_____

_____

Dad can write anything he wants.